"I'm so sorry."

Pocahontas, *Pocahontas*

SAY THE MAGIC WORDS

"I love you."

Belle, *Beauty and the Beast*

ATTITUDE COUNTS

Attitude
COUNTS

ATTITUDE COUNTS

"The very things
that held you down
are going to
carry you up."

Timothy Mouse, *Dumbo*

ATTITUDE COUNTS

"Nothing's impossible."

Doorknob, *Alice in Wonderland*

ATTITUDE COUNTS

"That's what
Rufus said:
Faith makes things
turn out right."

Penny, *The Rescuers*

ATTITUDE COUNTS

"I'm the only cat
of my kind."

O'Malley, *The Aristocats*

ATTITUDE COUNTS

"What do you do when things go wrong? Oh! You sing a song!"

Snow White, *Snow White and the Seven Dwarfs*

ATTITUDE COUNTS

"Things will look
better in the morning."

Bagheera, *The Jungle Book*

ATTITUDE COUNTS

"Hakuna matata
(no worries)!"

Pumbaa, *The Lion King*

ATTITUDE COUNTS

"Giving up is for rookies."

Phil, *Hercules*

ATTITUDE COUNTS

"The flower
that blooms in
adversity is the
most rare and
beautiful of all."

The Emperor, *Mulan*

ATTITUDE COUNTS

"I'm not worthless—and I don't have fleas."

Aladdin, *Aladdin*

ATTITUDE COUNTS

"Keep your chin up.
Someday there will
be happiness again."

Robin Hood, *Robin Hood*

ATTITUDE COUNTS

"To infinity and beyond!"

Buzz Lightyear, *Toy Story*

PLAY NICE

ADD A LITTLE MAGIC

PLAY NICE

"Share and share alike."

Happy, *Snow White and the Seven Dwarfs*

PLAY NICE

MANNERS MATTER

"March straight outside and wash, or you'll not get a bite to eat!"

Snow White, *Snow White and the Seven Dwarfs*

MANNERS MATTER

"Look up,
speak nicely,
& don't twiddle
your fingers."

Queen of Hearts, *Alice in Wonderland*

MANNERS MATTER

"If you can't say somethin' nice, don't say nothin' at all."

Thumper, *Bambi*

MANNERS MATTER

Manners

⚜

Matter

"Let's give whatever it is up there, a nice, big, Andy's room welcome."

Woody, *Toy Story*

PLAY NICE

"You helped me.
Now I will help you."

Quasimodo, *The Hunchback of Notre Dame*

PLAY NICE

"We've never had a cat
in our gang before,
but we can use all
the help we can get."

Fagin, *Oliver and Company*

PLAY NICE

"You must control your temper."

Lumiere, *Beauty and the Beast*

PLAY NICE

"At least
we should try to
get along together."

Cinderella, *Cinderella*

PLAY NICE

"The more
the merrier!"

Georges, *The Aristocats*

DON'T FORGET TO LAUGH

ADD A LITTLE MAGIC

DON'T FORGET TO LAUGH

"My bark is worse than my bite."

Grandmother Willow, *Pocahontas*

DON'T FORGET TO LAUGH

"Cheetahs never prosper."

Zazu, *The Lion King*

DON'T FORGET TO LAUGH

"Give me a hand."

Woody, *Toy Story*

DON'T FORGET TO LAUGH

"It appears that I now have an outlaw for an inlaw."

King Richard, *Robin Hood*

DON'T FORGET TO LAUGH

"One good turn deserves another."

Doorknob, *Alice in Wonderland*

DON'T FORGET TO LAUGH

"If it's not baroque,
don't fix it!"

Cogsworth, *Beauty and the Beast*

DON'T FORGET TO LAUGH

"Talk about your trunk space!"

The Genie, *Aladdin*

DON'T FORGET TO LAUGH

"That's our
lot in life.
It's not a lot,
but it's our life."

The Queen, *A Bug's Life*

MANNERS MATTER

"I just love
happy endings!"

Fauna, *Sleeping Beauty*

SURPRISES ARE AROUND THE CORNER

"Dry those
tears—you can't
go to the ball
looking like that."

The Fairy Godmother, *Cinderella*

SURPRISES ARE AROUND THE CORNER

"Little puppet
made of pine
WAKE!
The gift of life is thine."

Blue Fairy, *Pinocchio*

SURPRISES ARE AROUND THE CORNER

"We'll switch places
for a day."

The Prince, *The Prince and the Pauper*

SURPRISES ARE AROUND THE CORNER

"Looks like such
a beat-up worthless
piece of junk."

Aladdin, *Aladdin*

SURPRISES ARE AROUND THE CORNER

"Curiouser
and curiouser."

Alice, *Alice in Wonderland*

SURPRISES ARE AROUND THE CORNER

"They are
magic beans."

Mickey, *Mickey and the Beanstalk*

SURPRISES ARE AROUND THE CORNER

Surprises ARE AROUND EVERY CORNER

SURPRISES ARE AROUND THE CORNER

"There's a great
big hunk of world
down there, with
no fence around it."

Tramp, *Lady and the Tramp*

FOLLOW YOUR DREAMS

"Star light,
star bright,
First star I see tonight,
I wish I may,
I wish I might,
Have the wish
I wish tonight."

Geppetto, *Pinocchio*

FOLLOW YOUR DREAMS

"You gotta stay focused."

Phil, *Hercules*

FOLLOW YOUR DREAMS

"Are you ready to fly?"

Quasimodo, *The Hunchback of Notre Dame*

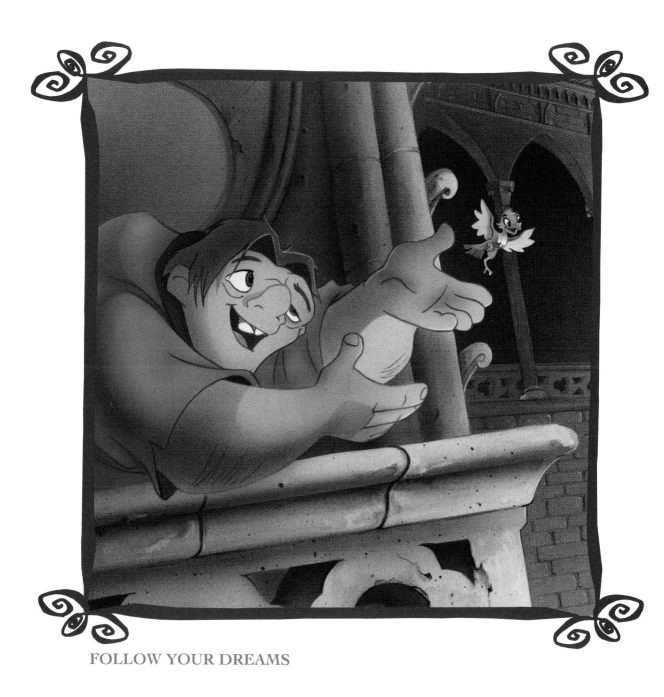

FOLLOW YOUR DREAMS

"Gain
self-confidence
by striking out
on your own."

Abigail Gabble, *The Aristocats*

FOLLOW YOUR DREAMS

"A dream is a wish your heart makes when you're fast asleep. In dreams you will lose your heartaches; whatever you wish for you keep. Have faith in your dreams and someday your rainbow will come smiling thru. No matter how your heart is grieving, if you keep on believing, the dream that you wish will come true."

"A Dream Is a Wish Your Heart Makes," *Cinderella*
Words & music by Mack David, Al Hoffman, & Jerry Livingston

FOLLOW YOUR DREAMS

"You don't have *time* to be timid—you must be bold, daring!"

Lumiere, *Beauty and the Beast*

FOLLOW YOUR DREAMS

"Life's not a spectator sport."

Laverne, *The Hunchback of Notre Dame*

BE YOURSELF

Follow
Your
Dreams

FOLLOW YOUR DREAMS

"Remember
who you are."

Mufasa, *The Lion King*

BE YOURSELF

"You can do it."

Thumper, *Bambi*

BE YOURSELF

"You know your path.
Now follow it."

Grandmother Willow, *Pocahontas*

BE YOURSELF

"Bee yourself."

The Genie, *Aladdin*

BE YOURSELF

"Just do your best."

Flora, *Sleeping Beauty*

ADD A LITTLE MAGIC

BE YOURSELF

"You're one
of a kind."

Hugo, *The Hunchback of Notre Dame*

BE YOURSELF

Be Yourself

BE YOURSELF

"Can't be
too careful,
you know."

Jiminy Cricket, *Pinocchio*

BEWARE OF BAD APPLES

"Now I'm warnin'
ya—don't let
nobody or nothin'
in the house."

BEWARE OF BAD APPLES

"Don't speak
to strangers."

Flora, *Sleeping Beauty*

BEWARE OF BAD APPLES

"The world is full
of temptations…
they're the
wrong things
that seem
right at the time."

Jiminy Cricket, *Pinocchio*

BEWARE OF BAD APPLES

Beware
of Bad Apples

BEWARE OF BAD APPLES

"A lie keeps growing and growing until it's as plain as the nose on your face."

Blue Fairy, *Pinocchio*

LISTEN AND LEARN

"I'm only brave
when I have to be. . .
Being brave doesn't
mean you go looking
for trouble."

Mufasa, *The Lion King*

LISTEN AND LEARN

"Darlin', forever is a long, long time, and time has a way of changin' things."

Big Mama, *The Fox and the Hound*

LISTEN AND LEARN

"Oh, to be free . . .
such a thing would be
greater than all the
magic and all the
treasures in the world!"

The Genie, *Aladdin*

LISTEN AND LEARN

"Don't spend your time just lookin' around for something you want that can't be found. When you find out you can live without it and go along not thinking about it, I'll tell you something true — the *bear* necessities of life will come to you."

"The Bear Necessities," *The Jungle Book*
Words & music by Terry Gilkyson

LISTEN AND LEARN

"We are
all connected
in the great
circle of life."

Mufasa, *The Lion King*

LISTEN AND LEARN

"A single grain of rice can tip the scale."

The Emperor, *Mulan*

LISTEN AND LEARN

"A true hero
isn't measured
by the size
of his strength,
but the strength
of his heart."

Zeus, *Hercules*

LISTEN AND LEARN

"Sometimes
the right path
is not the
easiest one."

Grandmother Willow, *Pocahontas*

LISTEN AND LEARN

"It is not
what is outside,
but what is inside
that counts."

Agrabah Salesman, *Aladdin*

LISTEN AND LEARN

Listen and LEARN

LISTEN AND LEARN

"The first thing in a visit is to state your name and business. Then shake hands."

Tweedledum, *Alice in Wonderland*

MANNERS MATTER

"Didn't your mother ever tell you not to play with your food?"

Zazu, *The Lion King*

MANNERS MATTER

"Ladies first."

Jim Dear, *Lady and the Tramp*

MANNERS MATTER

"We mustn't lurk in doorways—it's rude."

Ursula, *The Little Mermaid*

MANNERS MATTER

"Reflect before you act."

Mulan, *Mulan*

MANNERS MATTER

"It's very rude
to sit down
without
being invited."

March Hare, *Alice in Wonderland*

Disney's
Add a Little Magic

Words of Inspiration

Disney
PRESS

CONTENTS

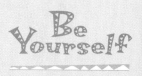

Magic
is everywhere
if you know
where to look…

...but if you're only watching for a Genie in a lamp or a Fairy Godmother with a magic wand, you're probably missing a whole lot of magic. Just ask your favorite Disney characters. They know that there's more to magic than a sprinkle of pixie dust or a "Bibbidi-bobbidi-boo." There's a special kind of magic in living your life the very best way you can— staying true to yourself, being good to others, and simply enjoying the world around you.

If you don't believe it, read on as Simba, Snow White, Pocahontas, Jiminy Cricket, Mulan, and many more of your favorite characters share what they know with you in their own words. And if you decide to follow their advice, don't be surprised if you start to notice more magic in your life!

SAY THE MAGIC WORDS

SAY THE MAGIC WORDS

"Please."

Sebastian, *The Little Mermaid*

SAY THE MAGIC WORDS

"Thank you."

Cinderella, *Cinderella*

SAY THE MAGIC WORDS